Nicola Walsh is an experienced teacher, school principal and schools' evaluator with over 30 years of international and UK-based experience in primary and early years education. She has served as a head teacher in the UK and as the principal of a large regional school in Sri Lanka. Nicola has inspected UK government schools, worked as an evaluator for the Ministry of Education in the UAE and as lead inspector for many British schools overseas. Working with charities and as a consultant she has advised and trained teachers in Cambodia, Egypt, India, Oman and Sri Lanka. Most recently she worked as the senior teacher for primary and early years for the British Council in Sri Lanka.

To my mother, my first teacher, and a teacher of everyone else.

Nicola Walsh

A Broad View of Educational Perspectives

AUSTIN MACAULEY PUBLISHERS™

LONDON ★ CAMBRIDGE ★ NEW YORK ★ SHARJAH

A CIP catalogue record for this title is available from the British Library.

ISBN 9781398494381 (Paperback)
ISBN 9781398494398 (ePub e-book)

www.austinmacauley.com

First Published 2023
Austin Macauley Publishers Ltd®
1 Canada Square
Canary Wharf
London
E14 5A

Acknowledgements

I would like to thank all the inspiring teachers I have worked with over the years.

A big thank you to my daughter who contributed very constructive advice before this book went to publication and gave me the confidence to go ahead. To the teachers at The Royal International School, Kurunegala, Sri Lanka and Kreu Yung school Ratanakiri province, Cambodia. Also, registered UK charity the TEA Project, Sri Lanka who placed me into some of the most challenging teacher training situations I had ever encountered. Finally, PENTA international, who continue to send me to very different schools in wide ranging contexts, where I meet amazing teachers and school leaders and of course, the children.

Table of Contents

Introduction

These articles were originally written as part of a monthly contribution to a leading business magazine in Sri Lanka. They were written to explain in simple terms, relevant educational issues for practitioners who do not speak English as their first language.

My experiences as a teacher, leader and inspector in many international and government schools helped to shape the articles. From the depths of the Cambodian jungle to deserted schools in the Arabian desert I drew upon my observations of teachers and their learners.

Each article is focused on the most recent thinking in education and includes references to relevant research and approaches. They are enhanced with useful anecdotes and examples, the how and why of teaching to anyone who is teaching using English as a second language.

Preface

A changing world, the importance of learning.

The world is changing, by the time you have read this sentence 20 more babies will have been born into a world where the future is changing at exponential rates. Students are being born into worlds where they are likely to have at least 10 different jobs before they are 38, where the technologies we are expecting them to use have not been invented yet, where life expectancy is likely to be beyond 100.

So, what does this tell our educators, our schools, our curriculum designers? How do we prepare students for the jobs we don't yet know exist, for technologies that have not yet been invented and into a world where change is commonplace. Where people are going to live longer, have more relationships and travel further?

Advances in technology mean that we no longer need to impart lists of facts and expect learners to memorise them and retain them for future use. Technology can give us the information we need at the touch of a button. Now learners need to be able to ask the right questions to get the information that they need. Asking questions, knowing where to go in a world of information overload becomes a much more important and useful skill than being able to recall the factors of 12.

Now, learners need to understand the process of learning so that as new technologies are invented, they can learn quickly and easily. Learning how to learn has increasing importance. Learning as a process is a useful tool to have in this world of constant change. If today's school students are likely to be working in different jobs, in different cultures, using different languages during their lifetime, the understanding of learning as a tool has a far greater significance than ever before. Alvin Toffler predicted: *the illiterate of the twenty-first century will not be those who cannot read and write, but those who cannot learn, unlearn and relearn.* (Toffler, 1971)

In the last decade of the twentieth century, discoveries in neuroscience increased the knowledge of how the brain develops and how we learn. This knowledge supported the earlier theories of learning such as those by Piaget, Bruner, Vygotsky, and Skinner.

Later, Professor Guy Claxton, the author of *Building Learning Power* (Claxton, 2002) detailed practical ideas about how to expand young people's capacity for learning. He advocated that teaching students how to learn empowered students to take charge of their own learning. Once students understood what they needed to do, they became better at managing distractions and to focus on the task. Students were taught explicitly to notice details in listening and looking. The whole language of learning became articulated and used as never before. Learning to learn, empowered learners.

A trend in action research resulted in books being published such as Doug Lemov's *Teach like a champion* (Lemov, 2010) and John Hattie's *Visible Learning* (Hattie, 2008). Observations of teaching and relevant collections of data meant that teachers became better informed around the science of learning.

However, access to this new information is restricted to educationalists who are fluent in English. This remains the preferred language of researchers, publishers and the internet. The world is changing, but English remains the most used second language.

Ensuring that the messages around teaching and learning are communicated simply and effectively so that everyone has a chance to learn, is the job of us all.

1. School Inspection

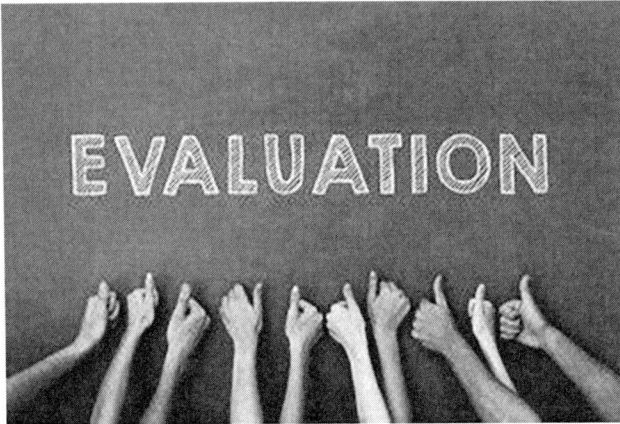

Should our schools be inspected? Does it make a difference? Inspection clearly matters, routine public inspections exist in other organisations. The health inspector, the police inspector, the building inspector are all instructed by governments to ensure that prescribed standards are maintained. So why not schools? Why have schools for so long acted in isolation with infrequent visits from inspectors?

Schools acted in isolation because inspection was difficult. How do you measure the effectiveness of the school or the impact of a teacher? Through testing, observation, questioning of the pupil? In 1870 a comment on the inspection of English Victorian schools noted: *The children of the village will be wise today because the inspector is visiting them. He will question them on their school subjects and, if they give the correct answers, he will give them the rest of the day off.[1] (Unknown, n.d.)'*

In the 1980s, UK education became a political bargaining tool resulting in a significant increase in teachers' salaries. This created the need for the government to justify and measure the impact of the increased education budget. Ultimately leading to a significant change in the inspection of schools. From 1992 UK schools were no longer going to be able to exist in 'glorious isolation'.

The introduction of the office for standards in education (Ofsted) and the 1992 Education Act (HMSO, 1992) gave inspectors the power to inspect all schools and to report judgements regarding the: *quality of education provided; the educational standards achieved by the schools' pupils; the efficiency of the use of resources; the spiritual, moral and cultural development of pupils.[2]* The Act placed a far greater emphasis on recording and reporting rather than the previous advisory role of inspection. To ensure consistency of judgements Ofsted created a common inspection framework. Now inspectors had a framework against which they would report a judgement regarding the effectiveness of a school. (Ofsted, 2019)

The framework determined expected standards, and this became a driving force for change across UK government-funded schools, which were now to be inspected routinely against a common framework and a judgement reported. No longer were schools operating unobserved. They were being compared and the judgements of the inspection visit published.

Has this led to change? Has this led to school improvement? Of course, schools had to ensure that the reported inspection judgements published were favourable. Otherwise, they risked falling pupil numbers and loss of staff.

---

[1] 1870 UK The National Archives

[2] Education (Schools) Act 1992 published Her Majesty's Stationery Office London 1992 (HMSO, 1992)

Quick to follow the UK's model were other countries. Australia favouring a self-evaluation model, wealthy overseas international schools developing their own models. The UK extended inspection to its' private schools and school's overseas. Inspection became a global phenomenon. *Inspections have won general acceptance and are perceived as a necessary accountability mechanism* (Ferguson, 2000).[3]

Why? Because school leaders and managers can measure the impact of their school against others. Private fee-paying schools value an inspection; if the results are favourable, the fees increased. Stakeholders recognise the multifaceted value of an external evaluation.

Inspection is a necessary driver of improvement in our schools. The detail of the inspection framework is an important factor in leading the direction of change. The more rigorous and frequent the inspection processes, the quicker the rate of change.

This in turn has led to greater visibility of the teacher's performance. A teacher is now accountable for the performance of the learners, the school leaders accountable for the performance of their teachers, and the school accountable for its performance to a funding body. Simple accountability.

But complicated at source. How do you measure the impact of a teacher on a child? It's easy for the police inspector to make a judgement; Is the crime solved? The building inspector; Is the building safe? The health inspector; Are premises hygienic? The school inspector; Is the school teaching its pupils?

Ferguson comments, *"It is too easy to overlook the fact that judgements in inspection reports are judgements and... are capable of a variety of interpretations that depend on the frame of reference and the previous experience of the individual inspector."*

Since the introduction of Ofsted in the UK, there has been a continual revision of the inspection process. The most notable changes being a steady

---

[3] *Improving schools and inspection.* Ferguson, N. Earley, P. Fifler, B. Ouston, J. 2000. Improving schools and inspection. London. Paul Chapman publishing.

decrease in notice period for schools and an increase in the purpose of school self-evaluation. Simultaneously schools have witnessed declining morale of staff, the increasing use of formal assessment, the loss of creativity in teaching styles, and the work of teachers being open to public scrutiny. This was recognised by the UK parliamentary subcommittee who in 1999 recommended to the Chief inspector of schools to be *'concerned to improve morale' in schools*. (Macbeath 2006)

So be cautious, inspection is a necessary driver of school improvement, it can be a useful tool to measure the effectiveness of a school and reduces the risk of schools operating in isolation. It informs governments and parents on the standards in their schools. But the process of school inspection must be implemented with care.

Questions for CPD sessions on chapter 1 School Inspection.

1. If inspecting schools is beneficial, describe why it may also be feared?
2. Explain how the process of inspection may lead to the demise of creativity.
3. Discuss the relevance of the quote: *'The children of the village will be wise today because the inspector is visiting.'*
4. Read together the section on grade descriptors in the UK schools inspection handbook and consider where your school would be judged.

https://www.gov.uk/government/publications/school-inspection-handbook-eif/school-inspection-handbook#part-3-grade-descriptors-for-graded-inspections

2. Why Attendance and Punctuality Matter

School register 1846

If school inspection makes a difference, then it is on school attendance that it has had the greatest impact. School principals in the UK became far more aware of the importance of the attendance and punctuality of their students once it was included in an inspection judgement.

Before inspection, no one seriously monitored the attendance of students. In fact, disruptive students were almost encouraged not to attend. Shopping centres were regular haunts of disengaged 15-year-old boys and girls on Friday afternoons. '*Skipping*' school was commonplace.

Following the adoption of the United Nations Convention on the Rights of the Child (UNCRC) in 1991 school attendance was given a greater focus, with reference to article 28.[4] Laws for the first time were enforced to ensure that children were in school and, more importantly, school attendance data became monitored. On inspection, if the inspector discovered that the attendance of students in a school fell below 95%[5] the school was given a weaker judgement and told to improve. As a result, principals monitored more closely the attendance of all students. The results were interesting. The students who were most likely to be absent were those who needed most to be in school. They were the lowest performing students, often with special educational needs. These were the children missing school!

More analysis of the attendance data revealed that if a student was absent in the first month of the school year, then this usually predicted low attendance for the remainder of the year. Setting a good habit in attendance in the first months of schooling really makes a difference.

UK research into links between attendance and performance in February 2015 (DfE, 2015), indicated that students with above 92% attendance rates in school are 1.6 times more likely to perform at an expected level in statutory tests than those students whose attendance fell below 85%. Internationally, other research data supports this view. Two days of non-attendance a month is equal to 10% absence, 4 days 20%. Poor attendance can influence whether children read proficiently by the end of third grade.[6] If a child cannot read, they cannot learn. When students increase their attendance rates, they improve their academic prospects and opportunities to access higher education.

Attendance in school not only allows students to learn but also to interact with other students and be safe. By enforcing attendance, students

---

[4] Article 28 1. States Parties recognize the right of the child to education, and with a view to achieving this right progressively and on the basis of equal opportunity, they shall, in particular: (a) Make primary education compulsory and available free to all;

[5] 95% is the expected attendance rate which allows 5% absence for common childhood illnesses

[6] Grade 3 = Pupils aged 8 or 9 years

are safe. In school, they are monitored by peers, teachers and parents know where they are. Students who are not in school are at risk of harm. Students who are regular non-attenders are much more likely to get into trouble outside the home. (Taylor, 2012)

Punctuality enforces good discipline. Teachers embed in students a strong work ethic that is valued, by teachers and their peers. Students who arrive late to lessons not only miss out on the introduction of the lesson but disrupt the learning of others. Preventing others from learning is disrespecting every child's right to learn.

Recently, meeting with a group of regional advisors in a developing country, their response to the reason why students do not attend school was surprising. They said students do not attend school because they are poor. They seemed to be unaware of the UNCRC article 28; every child has a right to attend school, rich or poor. Governments should follow UN guidance and *'take appropriate measures to encourage regular attendance at schools and the reduction of drop-out rates'* (UNICEF, 1989)

Poverty should not be allowed to be a factor that determines whether a child attends school or not. If the family is poor, then the school must do everything it can to ensure the child attends school. Research has shown that students who live in communities with high levels of poverty are four times more likely to be chronically (long term) absent than others. Often for reasons beyond their control, such as unstable housing, unreliable transportation, and a lack of access to health care. Schools and their principals must work with families to address these issues in the communities if poverty is to be eradicated.

I recently worked with a principal in a school where classrooms were almost empty. It was an easy to school to manage as a principal when most students are absent. When I suggested that attendance be monitored and the children asked to attend school, the principal could not see the reason why. Staff were being paid. The principal did not see that it was an essential and fundamental part of the role; to improve student attendance by engaging students and parents in positive ways and providing support.

Only when governments set clear policies that make attendance of students in school a priority, will attendance change. This needs to be a shift from measuring how many are on the school's admission register. Working in a remote region of southeast Asia in rural village schools, it became apparent that the students (and teachers) only turned up to school on the days the inspectors visited!

Principals must understand and be accountable for the attendance of students in their schools. Then we will see full classrooms, a reduction in the crime rate among young offenders and a potential increase in life chances for the poorest people.

Questions for CPD sessions on chapter 2 Why Attendance and Punctuality Matter.

1. If attitudes towards punctuality can be attributed to different cultural expectations, how would you manage this?
2. Discuss the many ways that students who are not in school are at risk.
3. If increasing attendance increase life chances, then why is it not a priority in all schools?
4. Consider your schools' attendance data and highlight which classes, grades and individuals are not attending school for 95% of the school year.

3. Becoming a Leader

Chandler, 1840

Leaders are great people, it's a lonely job and there's no going back. In a traditional tale, Chicken Licken was a convincing leader and others happily followed. But the vision was not shared or clear and ultimately Chicken Licken led her followers into the fox's den. Make sure you know where you are going at the outset. Then get others to follow.

Anyone taking up a new leadership role at the start of the year needs to have a clear vision of what they want to achieve beyond the end of the year, in fact, think in terms of a contract. Also, take time to audit what's in place before making any changes.

Becoming a leader is a challenge. It means that someone has recognised an ability to lead. Don't ever forget that. Be wary, advice will be forthcoming, and the trick is to listen to it all and rely upon instinct. That's why you have secured the role because someone believes you have the ability to lead and not necessarily those around you.

However, actively seek their views of others. Ask for feedback by asking questions of all your team, at all levels, not just those who are most keen to give it. They will be grateful you are asking for their views. And listen. Carefully.

Never think you know it all. Actively show you are learning too. As a school principal in Sri Lanka, I learnt to dress in a saree and wore it regularly to school. As a westerner it caused a great deal of mirth, I had many, many offers of help to improve my dressing skills and my teachers taught me. It became a reciprocal relationship. Be humble, show what you don't know and be willing to learn from those around you.

Build a strong team by employing people who know more than you. Show others that you rely upon their experience and knowledge to help you make the tough decisions. I regularly see long-serving school leaders, appointing much younger inexperienced staff as they are fearful of conflict. A real shame for the school, as it weakens the school's capacity to improve through healthy challenges and debate. With a team of experienced, critically evaluating, and passionate staff on your team, who have a joint vision and want to see the organisation improve, changes will happen. As David Ogilvy said to advertising executives in 1985, "If each of us hires people who are smaller than we are, we shall become a company of dwarves, but if each of us hires people who are bigger than we are, we shall become a company of giants". (Ogilvy, 1985)

Remember as the person at the top you ultimately hold the authority, but don't let power get in your way. The greatest leaders lead from within. Exerting power over others is no longer the way to lead. I have seen leaders frequently beat staff with the threat of the consequences of underperformance. But that's not the way to develop high performers who

23

believe in a shared vision and are committed long term. Where there is underperformance, seek out the reasons why and address it. That way staff feel supported, and this eliminates the climate of fear.

Once you recognise the abilities in others, enable them to use them. Howard Schulz transformed Starbucks Coffee Company in the 1980s by believing that "People want guidance, not rhetoric. They need to know what the plan of action is, and how it will be implemented. They want to be given responsibility to help solve the problem and authority to act on it." (Schultz, 1997) He set up an organisation where people's contributions were seen as potential solutions to the problems and not the problem.

Poorly motivated and uninspired people can be the downfall of even the most amazing organisations. Leadership is key in empowering individuals to have the knowledge, skill, desire, and opportunity to personally succeed in a way that leads to collective organisational success. Being able to develop a team of people who devote their efforts entirely to the co-operative effort of the team is a highly valued skill.

So be prepared to learn, relearn, and unlearn and be a positive team player. Don't rush into leadership too soon. How can you expect others to be responsive to your comments if they don't believe you can do it too? Many professionals rise quickly to the top, admonish others for underperformance but haven't experienced how to do it themselves.

Ensure your experience is relevant and use it to lead. Lead with a shared clear vision of where you want to go and empower others to help you. You are all on the same journey, they are the drivers too, be prepared to share the wheel.

Questions for CPD sessions on chapter 3 Becoming a Leader.

1. Outline the differences between leaders and managers.
2. Describe how the author built relationships and led from within. Why was this approach important?

3. Chicken Licken is a children's story. Highlight the importance of building leadership skills in young people and how traditional tales may help you to do this.

4. Investing in Education

A global learning crisis: The expected learning outcomes
of the cohort of children and youth who are of school age in 2030

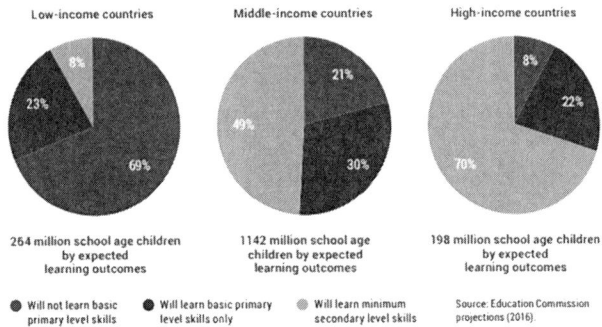

Low-income countries	Middle-income countries	High-income countries
8% / 23% / 69%	21% / 49% / 30%	8% / 22% / 70%
264 million school age children by expected learning outcomes	1142 million school age children by expected learning outcomes	198 million school age children by expected learning outcomes

● Will not learn basic primary level skills   ● Will learn basic primary level skills only   ● Will learn minimum secondary level skills

Source: Education Commission projections (2016).

https://report.educationcommission.org/wp-content/uploads/2016/09/Learning_Generation_Full_Report.pdf

Investment is a commitment to achieving the desired outcome. In education, the desired outcome is to ensure all students learn.

'Increasing educational attainment by a single grade level boosts lifetime income by 10-20% for girls and 5-15% for boys. If all students in low-income countries left school with basic reading skills, 171 million people could be lifted out of poverty, which is equivalent to a 12% drop in global poverty.

Yet, 550 million children around the globe are failing to receive a quality 21st century education. There are 340 million students of school-

going age not in school, and many children who are in school never achieve basic numeracy or literacy: **50% are failed by underperforming systems**. (UNESCO, 2017)

So, what are the characteristics of effective education systems in which governments should be investing?

Attendance in school. If a learner does not attend lessons, then the teacher has little chance of teaching them effectively. Attendance in school must be rigorously monitored at class, school, regional and government levels. Actions must be taken against learners who do not attend. School leaders can only monitor and report, they require authorities to ensure that the learner recognises that attendance is expected. 95% attendance is the expected standard in the UK, below this is a concern. *'Days off cost good grades.' 'Attend today, achieve tomorrow.'* Both tag lines are used by American schools to remind learners of the benefits of good attendance.

Training teachers at the start of their careers on best international practice is essential. Training needs to include what teachers teach (the curriculum), how they deliver (teaching methods) and the importance of preparation (planning and assessment). There needs to be a radical shift away from the theories of learning. Teacher training must aim to improve teacher subject knowledge, assessment methods, and practical skills in the classroom. This investment will create effective teachers.

Investment needs to see a return. The impact of the investment in training is measured in outcomes for learners. **Teachers must therefore routinely monitor the progress and attainment of all learners**. So that there is a clear link between investment in training teachers and the rates of progress and attainment levels of learners. Teachers must be trained to monitor progress, measure attainment, and compare this against other cohorts, schools and regions. Governments need to be monitoring the performance of their learners against international benchmarks.

Investing in research and development, creating teacher forums, or networks that allow teachers to discuss their practice and share ideas have positive impacts on those that engage. This is a low-cost method and often is very effective at changing behaviours. In-service training of teachers ensures that teachers are trained in the classroom and can quickly adapt and try out new ideas. It ensures consistency of practice and ensures a minimum standard, if there is an expectation that all engage.

Keeping children safe. Leaders and teachers must be trained to monitor the well-being of all learners in school and in the wider communities. Learners will not learn if they feel threatened or anxious. Research underpins this. (Maslow, 1943) Many learners in poor communities arrive at school willing to learn but arrive with barriers to learning; neglect, hunger, and abuse at home. Most people who have attended school in the past will know of one learner who failed to thrive because of issues that were ignored by the school. Investing in the well-being of all our learners is a moral obligation in our schools. It is one that needs to be monitored and acted upon seriously by school leaders in countries where education levels are low. Every child must have access to education and barriers to this removed.

There needs to be more **accurate monitoring of individual school performances** by governments. As schools become more directly accountable for the performances of their learners, they become more committed to invest in developing teachers. Investment is hindered in many countries by parent's use of tutors. Schools may achieve outstanding results in external examinations although the quality of teaching is poor. In many cases this is due to the investment by parents in employing the use of a tutor after school. This masks a school's performance and is not easily affordable by all. Every child matters; if we are going to improve life chances for everyone, not just those who can afford tutors.

In summary, investment is essential to ensure those in the profession are well equipped to make a positive difference to the lives of those that they teach. Schools and their leaders must be accountable for the quality of teaching in their school and the outcomes for learners. This includes a duty on the school to ensure the well-being of all learners and teachers, alongside continued monitoring and reporting on attendance.

If we are to increase the numbers of children receiving a twenty-first century education, then 'Every Teacher Matters'.

Questions for CPD sessions on chapter 4 Investing in Education.

1. For your school or educational setting, consider the 6 points of effective teaching. Which one does your school do best?
2. Describe the desired outcome of effective teaching. Is this the same for every school?
3. How can you invest in keeping children safe?

5. Effective Teaching

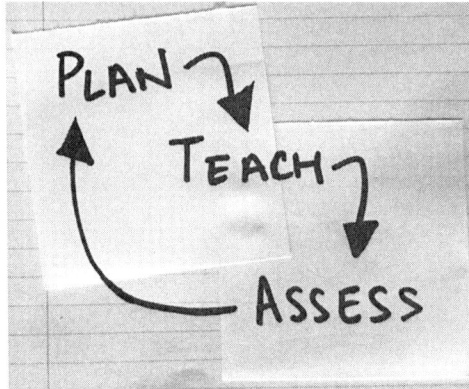

My father taught me to drive a car. He was an effective teacher, but the learning was hard. He was not a trained teacher. He was determined that I should succeed and despite the lack of lesson plans, learning objectives and three-part lesson, I passed the first time. As his daughter was involved, he was fully committed to achieving success.

Some approaches to teaching come naturally and others are acquired. Training teachers should ensure that the learning is easy and that outcomes are successful. Here are four attributes shared by effective teachers:

The first is being organised.

Organised in what you are going to teach, what you are going to do, in your preparation, the acquisition of resources, the delivery of the materials and the organisation of the very important space, the classroom. Lessons are planned and teachers are organised in what they want the learners to learn. Lesson objectives are progressive and deliver the curriculum material in an organised approach.

The second is monitoring the progress of the learners. An effective teacher does this naturally and it is ongoing.

An effective teacher uses the learning objective to monitor the understanding of the learners *at the beginning, during* and *at the end* of the teaching.

They check understanding by ASKING QUESTIONS. Sometimes called 'formative assessment' because it informs. Teachers who don't ask questions are called LECTURERS. They deliver and walk away. An effective teacher asks questions routinely and checks the understanding of the learners against the objective. Where there is a misunderstanding effective teachers address it.

Effective teachers MARK BOOKS. They monitor the understanding through careful analysis of the learner's responses and give feedback that promotes progress. They monitor the quality and quantity of work and monitor improvements in understanding over time.

Effective teachers formally assess learners and compare this to previous results, other learners, cohorts, schools, countries. Comparisons are used to monitor progress and attainment.

Great teachers monitor learners who fail to make progress and set appropriate work to ensure these learners make progress and catch up. Some learners make quick progress and some struggle to make any. With the appropriate tasks set any learner can make progress over time.

The third characteristic of effective teaching is possibly the hardest to acquire. Commanding respect.

This is an equally mutual attribute between teacher and learner. Some teachers believe this to be one way, where learners are expected to respect teachers, without question. However, respect should be earned by both parties; the teacher respects the learner, understands their strengths and weaknesses and is committed to ensuring the learner is successful.

A great teacher will discover in every learner their strengths and use these to build on the areas of weakness in that particular learner.

A great teacher isn't afraid to guide students. Learners appreciate teachers who challenge and set high standards. Know your learners thoroughly and this inspires respect.

Finally, the last characteristic and the most important is **the ability of the teacher to be reflective**. An effective teacher continually reflects on their own practice. They actively seek feedback with the aim to improve provision for all learners.

When a learner fails to understand or make progress a reflective teacher will be actively considering, *is there a better way?* The teacher will create other approaches to engage and make the learning easy. A reflective teacher will always self-reflect. When a learner doesn't understand, it's the fault of the teacher and not the learner.

Effective teachers talk with other teachers and share good ideas and approaches. Staff rooms are vital to ensuring this takes place. An improved vocabulary regarding the pedagogy of teaching has facilitated this over recent years. Teachers learn best when talking about what they do, by imitating others and continually reviewing and revising.

So, these are the four basic characteristics of effective teachers. These are reflected in the UK Teachers Standard (DfE UK, 2011) and a report by The Education Endowment Federation (Foundation, 2022). They led research in the UK into which approach by schools had the most impact on learners. In the USA researcher Doug Lemov adopted a sensible approach to simply observe great teachers. From this, he created a list of the common attributes. He wrote a list of 49 attributes of great teachers. This list is a useful tool for those of us who wish to train effective teachers. He wrote a book based on his observations *Teach Like a Champion* (Lemov, 2010) it's worth a read, even if you are a busy teacher, make time for it.

Finally, I revert to the beginning image of the effective teacher, my father teaching me to drive. There is a teacher in all of us. He was successful because he was driven by emotional involvement with the learner. However, he struggled to make the learning easy as he had not been trained. Passionate, qualified teachers should be making the learning easy and ensuring every learner succeeds. Teaching isn't hard. Effective teaching is achievable. Teachers must be fully committed to achieving successful outcomes for every individual learner and making the learning easy.

Questions for CPD sessions on chapter 5 Effective Teaching.

1. Is there a teacher within all of us? Discuss.
2. What are the links between promoting teachers to talk and leading from within?
3. Explain why being a reflective teacher is an important part of being effective.

Using the Observation Checklist shown below, create a written definition of effective teaching.

Observation Checklist:

Classroom environment	Yes	No	Comments
Does the arrangement of the classroom allow every child to sec the whiteboard?			
Does the arrangement of the classroom reduce visual & noise distractions for the children?			
Can the teacher and students move around the classroom easily?			
Do displays support leaming?			

	All	Majority	Few/none
Are there support materials? Word lists, number lines.			
Are there reading books available?			
Pupils	**All**	**Majority**	**Few/none**
Do children have necessary equipment and books?			
Do children look at the teacher or whiteboard as she is teaching?			
Do children settle to the independent tasks quickly?			
Do children complete the tasks set in the time given?			
Do children have an opportunity to contribute their ideas?			
Do children ask questions of the teacher about the lesson content?			
Do children talk to one another about the content of the lesson?			
Do children continue to talk about the lesson content after the lesson has finished?			
Are children busy all the time?			
Do children have strategies to seek support?			
Can pupils explain confidently and clearly what they have learnt.			
Can pupils understand what they need to do to improve?			
Can pupils judge their own work and that of others and give suggestions as to how it can be improved?			

6. Marking and Feedback

George Cruickshank British cartoonist 1792 – 1878

What has the greatest influence on the outcomes of learners? What really makes a difference when we are teaching students?

Feedback: The teacher's individual response to the learner upon completion of a task has been well documented as having the greatest influence on learners. As early as 1924 Pressey, a leading psychologist into human behaviour at Ohio State University invented the teaching machine. (Benjamin, 1988). It was a machine that administered multiple choice questions to students, the machine was fixed so that the student could not progress until selecting the right answer. Pressey recognised that by giving feedback in the form of the correct answer to a student then learning took place. Later Skinner in the 1940s, recognising the value of feedback advertised his teaching machine; *'Reinforcement for the right answer is immediate'*. Unfortunately, its use was short-lived as it was cumbersome, expensive and required the administrative efforts of a teacher. Today computers are doing much the same. Instant feedback reaps rewards.

Research in 2011 by Education Endowment (Foundation, 2022) Foundation , showed that of 34 factors considered, feedback has a very high effect on learners. *'High impact for a very low cost'*. Recently John Hattie (Hattie, 2008) attempted a visible measure of *'What has the greatest effect on student learning?'* and top of his list is feedback. Hattie suggested that with effective feedback a learner can make over one year's gain in learning. He cautions, *Feedback is one of the most powerful influences on learning and achievement, but this impact can be either positive or negative.* So, we need to ensure it is used positively if it is to have the greatest benefit.

We can all remember the negative consequences of the feedback Oliver Twist received in the novel by Dickens when he asked for more gruel. *"Please sir," replied Oliver, "I want some more." The master aimed a blow at Oliver's head with the ladle and pinioned him in his arms and shrieked aloud for the beadle.* Maybe we all have memories of a teacher whose feedback was detrimental to our progress but let's dwell on the positives.

Feedback is the communication of praise, criticism, or advice to a learner. It can be spoken, written, or non-verbal. It is common in schools in a variety of forms. Questions are essential. Oliver asked a question, and he got the feedback. Teachers ask questions to ascertain the understanding of students. Students ask questions of the teacher. Questioning is a useful tool to generate feedback however the most established form of regular feedback in schooling is marking by the teacher.

The marking of exercise books is a daily and onerous task. Good teachers realise the benefits and complete marking without delay. Without this form of feedback, how are learners to know if their efforts to record their learning are accurate or more importantly inaccurate?

Further to enable teachers to plan teaching matched to ability, teachers must mark the books. Where a teacher comments 'try again …' indicates that the teacher has recognised that the student has not fully understood. Conversely, pages full of correct work indicate that the tasks set lack challenge, it's too easy. Where the teaching is well matched there is a balance of errors and success.

Further by monitoring the feedback of the whole class, a teacher can seek information about the effectiveness of the teaching. When errors occur across a class of students the teacher needs to rethink the approach, it's not the fault of the students.

So, marking gives feedback to the teacher on the quality of their teaching and the understanding of the learners. How useful is that?

Marking doesn't need to be detailed for every task, but it needs to be done. It needs to be completed no matter how minimal the task. Students need feedback on spelling tests, table tests, writing and math's work. They need to know that their presentation is good enough. A teacher can set standards if work is marked routinely. Work can be DONE AGAIN if the standard reached is not good enough!

All this said, feedback can only be effective if the student is receptive. How many times is feedback ignored? A clever teacher will pose questions and expect an answer. This way the teacher knows that hours spent marking are having an impact. 'Can you think of a better way to…?' writes the teacher. 'Write out three times…' and spelling errors are eradicated. This culture of response is promoted by the teacher.

The importance of work produced by students has a high priority in monitoring the performance of a school. Senior leaders and evaluators can quickly ascertain the strengths of a teacher on the quality of the work in books and the quality of the feedback given. If work produced over time evidence progress, then that's the sign of a good teacher. A student who receives quality feedback routinely and regularly is going to make more progress than a student who doesn't. Guaranteed.

Questions for CPD sessions on chapter 6 Marking and Feedback.

1. Consider, how often do you mark your students work and do you expect them to respond?
2. Discuss, which is strongest verbal or written feedback?
3. 'The more mistakes you make, the more you learn.' How can that statement impact on your behaviours as a teacher?

4. Using a full set of students' exercise books copy and complete the work scrutiny checklist below.

Exercise Book Checklist for Primary/Elementary Schools

Presentation	Always	Sometimes	Rarely	Never
Is work dated? Written in full in English, Science, GK, Topic & Science books.				
Is work given a clear title or learning objective?				
Is work in order and on every page, no gaps?				
Is work underlined before starting the next piece of work?				
Are pages intact and the book named clearly on the front?				
Feedback				
Is work marked?				
Are there marking comments from the teacher?				
Do the marking comments help the child to improve?				

Are spelling and punctuation errors corrected?				
Can the teachers handwriting be read easily?				
Do the students respond to the teachers marking comments?				
Quantity				
Is there enough work for one lesson?				
Is work produced daily in English and maths?				
Is work produced weekly in other subjects?				
Variety				
Is there evidence of different work to match the abilities of the students in one lesson?				
Is there more challenging work for clever children?				
Is there evidence of support for children who find the work difficult?				
Does the work produced show a variety of ways of recording learning? (Diagrams, Writing, tables, charts)				
Does the work show a lively, imaginative curriculum?				

7. Can Students Be Teachers?

Rohwer Relocation Center, McGehee, Arkansas. Lily Namimoto, teacher.
Student teachers in second grade class.
https://www.archives.gov/college-park

I recently had the privilege to be a school inspector and observed classrooms with teachers and students interacting. In one such case, I observed a group of three students working together, the task had been set by the teacher and each pupil within the group had a clear role in the deployment of the task, as reader, writer, and speaker. I watched with interest; the students worked very effectively to resolve the task by each taking on their assigned roles. They got through the task quicker than they had been working independently, were well motivated and worked extremely well collaboratively, listening and articulating the problem. Are they teachers? No, but they are working together to solve a task. This is a significant shift from the competitive individualised learning environments of classrooms I see in so many schools.

Another example that does support the notion that students can be effective teachers again I observed on an inspection visit. Here students were sat in mixed ability groups in a math's class working on different problems, when they were struggling to resolve the task, they FIRST sought the help of the student next to them. Clearly, the most able pupil in the group was going to be helping most to explain to a fellow student how to resolve a problem. However, this is a skill and one worth developing. When there is only one teacher in a class of 30 students and the pupil who seeks help waits for the attention of the teacher valuable learning time is lost. Here I felt that peers were effective and again students completed tasks by talking to one another in an environment that is mutually supportive. *'Check your Book, ask your Buddy and then ask the Boss'*

In both examples, students were not grouped by ability and learners were not discovering new ideas by themselves. The teacher had presented the task and by careful design facilitated cooperative learning.

Let's consider why don't students make effective teachers. To be an effective teacher you must know your subject well, you must understand the abilities of your students, identify misconceptions and tailor the lesson content to match the abilities of the students. Your delivery is key to motivating students and having a clear success criterion so you as a teacher are clear about what you want the students to learn and can benchmark progress against this.

Can students do this? Some students can quickly and rapidly gain mastery of the subject. They also know the abilities of their peers. (I have not yet been in an established classroom where the students are not able to easily identify the clever students and the not-so-clever students.) Students are very perceptive about the abilities of their peers.

Conversely, students are not experienced at delivering effective lessons, knowing what to teach based on a prescribed curriculum and using feedback to measure progress. All these areas are the domains of a trained teacher, so I am not advocating we replace teachers with students!

But upskilling students to support one another, to work in an environment that is mutually supportive and develop the skills of speaking and listening and collaboration is fundamentally a good thing. We all want to live in environments where we effectively work together to support one another and improve our knowledge. A move away from competitive classrooms, where students compete against one another for the exclusive A+ and become individualised in their learning and acquisition of knowledge, is surely a positive change.

Teachers need to recognise this and consider cooperative learning methods. First, students need to feel safe but also challenged. Second, groups need to be small enough that everyone can contribute. Third, the task students work together on must be clearly defined. So, the role of the teacher is still important, but the traditional method is changing. Teachers need to take stock of what American anthropologist and humanist Ashley Montague wrote in 1956;

"Without the cooperation of its members, society cannot survive, and the society of man has survived because the cooperativeness of its members made survival possible... It was not an advantageous individual here and there who did so, but the group. In human societies, the individuals who are most likely to survive are those who are best enabled to do so by their group." (Montague, 1966)

Further, the benefits of cooperative learning are well documented in recent research: *'Cooperative Learning promotes deep learning of course materials through a diversity of perspectives fostered by interactions between peers... students achieve better grades in cooperative learning than in competitive or individual learning* (Shimazoe, 2010)'. So yes, students are effective teachers when they are allowed to work cooperatively.

Questions for CPD sessions on chapter 7 Can Students Be Teachers?

1. What classroom management strategies might you employ after reading this chapter?
2. Discuss. Developing students' skills in speaking, listening and collaboration are more important than subject content.
3. Are students disadvantaged when working in ability groups?

8. Critical Thinking, What Does It Mean?

We hear a lot about the 4 C's in education: Communication, Collaboration, Creativity, and Critical thinking. These are the skills we must ensure our students possess, as Barrack Obama said in his speech to the Hispanic Chamber of Commerce in March 2009:

"I'm calling on our nation's governors and state education chiefs to develop standards and assessments that don't simply measure whether students can fill in a bubble on a test, but whether they possess twenty-first-century skills like problem-solving, critical thinking, entrepreneurship and creativity (Obama, 2009)."

So how do we develop these twenty-first-century skills in our students and in our teachers? The first 3 C's, communication, collaboration and creativity are relatively easy to facilitate in a classroom, however, the development of critical thinking as a skill requires careful consideration. Not least because there are a variety of different interpretations of what this term means. Research, revealed that instructors teaching critical thinking do not have a clear understanding of what critical thinking means, and Pearson's (2017) *Skills for Today* (Ventura, 2017) reports that 'instructors still struggle with what critical thinking actually means.

Further promoters of the importance of critical thinking cannot agree on the importance of background knowledge. Some argue that without a basic mastery of subject knowledge it's impossible to be able to think critically. Conversely, others believe the dispositions required to think critically can be acquired with very limited banks of knowledge. Is it a disposition or a skill? There is no strong consensus.

However, there are elements common to all definitions. Simply put, we need to be creating learners who can ask questions about the information they are given, using the knowledge they must think beyond the task and work independently. They need to be critical about the source of knowledge and check sources routinely before making judgements and taking decisions.

Let's look at thinking first. Robert Fisher (Fisher, 2013), a leading expert in developing students' thinking skills, says that thinking is not a natural function like sleeping, walking and talking. Thinking, he stresses, is a skill that needs to be developed. Students need to be taught to think explicitly. Teachers need to be training students to think. In a modern 21st century classroom, teachers must facilitate time for thinking to happen and model it themselves. 'Let me think about that…' Understanding how we learn, skills in metacognition are important in helping how this happens. Skills such as resilience, reciprocity, resourcefulness and reflectivity need to be developed. Concentration can be developed through practice. Board games, sporting activities, learning a musical instrument, reading and puzzles at the right level of ability can extend a learner's ability to focus.

Questioning is key to developing within a child an enquiring mind. Encouraging students to ask questions develops an enquiring mind. Adults who ask students questions they do not themselves have the answer to, recognise the value of the child's thinking. The child can see that the adult is taking them seriously. Asking questions such as *'How are we going to do this? What's the best way to get this problem sorted?'*

Being critical. Developing a curious mind that questions how and why has always been the mission of a good teacher. Now we must ensure that teachers develop within learners a critical attitude to knowledge. Learners need to routinely question the reliability of the evidence. Are you sure? How do you know that's true? Teachers must model critical attitudes to knowledge so that learners know to consider the source and reliability of the evidence, to evaluate the claims made considering the evidence given before making an informed judgement or decision.

Good teachers can facilitate critical attitudes to new knowledge and develop thinking as a skill. Both are more important than the subject through which they are taught. Ninety-five percent of the chief academic officers from 433 higher-education institutions rated critical thinking as one of the most important skills for students to acquire (Association of American Colleges and Universities, 2011). (Hart Research Associates, 2013)

In the twenty-first century, subject knowledge can be sourced easily, it is now the job of a teacher to use the subject content to facilitate critical attitudes and thinking skills. Encourage learners to reason effectively, think of systems as part of a whole, make judgements, decisions and solve problems. Learners have to be able to see the bigger picture and connect the purpose of the learning to real life. In PE it's no longer acceptable to be able to learn to kick a ball, learners need to be able to consider; How far will it go? What will the impact be? And is there a better way?

As American president F.D. Roosevelt once said, *"We cannot build the future for our youth, but we can build our youth for the future."* We need to start building our youth, and our teachers, to think critically.

Questions for CPD sessions on chapter 8 Critical Thinking. What does it mean?

1. How can you promote critical thinking behaviours in your lessons?
2. Discuss the meaning of *"We cannot build the future for our youth, but we can build our youth for the future."*
3. Write a set of questions to use to develop critical thinking strategies in your students.

9. Gender Issues in Education

Girls and boys come out to play,
the moon does shine as bright as day,
Leave your supper and leave your sleep,
And come with your playfellows into the street.

– Old English nursery rhyme

Girls generally outperform boys at school. From an early age, girls do better. They arrive at school ready to learn, sit still and listen. Boys are physically active and take longer to settle into academic work. Programme for International Student Assessment (PISA) (OECD, n.d.) [7] scores show that girls in all 65 countries do better at age 15 than boys in reading. So why is there a difference?

Simply put, the brains' of boys and girls are not the same. Even before birth, our brains are distinctly different. Although the brains of a foetus are identical for the first 12 weeks. At three months, the male foetus receives a high dose of androgens, a chemical that causes significant changes in the brain. Much later at puberty, hormones are released that create different levels of chemicals so that male and female brains develop differently. Clearly, there is a continuum, and the levels of difference vary. Some male brains may be very female and conversely, some female brains may be more masculine than others.

---

[7] PISA Programme for International Student Assessment. Pupils aged 15, average scores in mathematics, science and reading by country. (OECD, n.d.)

Our brains are divided into two hemispheres, the left side processes analytical, logical linguistic concepts and the right side, global non-verbal concepts. Generally, men tend to use only one hemisphere of their brains at any one time – therefore men are focused and less aware of distractions. Whereas females find it easier to multitask. This is because the female brain has a bigger corpus callosum, which is a bridge of fibres that links the left and right hemispheres together. Therefore, girl's brains are more integrated and both hemispheres are active simultaneously.

Most males have a larger area of the brain devoted to visual and spatial processing that's why they enjoy music, solving 3D puzzles, construction toys, football and cartoons. Whereas a female brain has a larger left side which is the area used for linguistic processing. As a result, most girls learn to talk, read and write earlier than males, therefore they make rapid progress in building social relationships and learning from one another.

It is well known that males have a higher level of testosterone, the hormone that causes humans to be action orientated, competitive and aggressive. Boys need to actively explore the space around them and will work hard to be the first in any challenge. Whereas girls, with lower levels of testosterone, are more co-operative, less concerned with winning and more involved in processes. They are less likely to explore, instinctively willing to use their energies to create a safe home environment ready to raise their young.

Parents of boys will tell you how much harder they are to discipline than girls, that is because males have lower levels of serotonin, a chemical used to engage the logical and rational parts of the brain. As a result, boys find it harder to control their behaviours without clear boundaries. This may be the reason why most pupils expelled from schools are boys. Higher levels of serotonin in female brains enable girls to be rational and make the right decisions without the influence of others. Ironically, parents are usually stricter with girls which may contribute further to girls having higher levels of self-control.

Dopamine is a chemical that alerts the brain to important information. High endorphin levels can boost dopamine production. Triggering endorphin release into the body can be achieved through increased exercise. Boys have less dopamine than girls, so making them play rugby or participate in any exercise before class will help them to focus. Girls don't need to do this as they have higher levels of dopamine.

So, can differences in our brains account for the different behaviours? Girls generally are less aggressive, peace-making, literate and cooperative. Boys, generally are explorative, active and risk takers.

Boys still underperform overall because the methods teachers adopt in all schools are very similar. Where teaching and learning have an emphasis on tasks that are cooperative and non-competitive, sedentary and requiring sustained attention, the girls do better.

Male and female brains are biologically different and therefore learn in different ways. If teachers learn to recognise these differences, they might be able to consider activities that offer some hope for the boys. Girls thrive in a traditional teaching setting and can learn in any environment. But the boys need dynamic lessons, with short amounts of teacher talk followed by tasks that are active, competitive and challenging. Think of action/adventure movies, camera, lights, action, and less writing.

There are no differences in terms of what boys and girls can learn, in fact, boys have the capacity to learn more due to their curious nature and competitive drive to seek out knowledge. But there are big differences in the methods that are used effectively to teach the different genders. Currently, our teaching methods favour girls, therefore girls do better.

Questions for CPD sessions on chapter 9 Gender Issues in Education.

1. What methods and approaches can you employ in your teaching that will engage boys fully, and promote equality of both boys and girls?

2. Discuss advertising and the differences in content when the product is aimed at a specific gender.

3. How can you teach PE to a mixed secondary class and ensure the girls have equal opportunities as the boys to be successful?

10. Gifted or Talented?

Since the beginning of the twentieth century, there has been increased interest in the identification and provision for students whose performance levels are significantly beyond that expected for their age. The search to identify students whose abilities are above those of the norm is not a new idea. In the fourth century BC, Plato set up in Athens an academy to provide a stimulus for the most able students and in the Tang dynasty of 560–618 child prodigies were identified and given a special place at court.

In the 1920s and '30s, research work by psychologists such as Terman and Hollingworth (Robinson, 2013) investigated the concept that a few students are more intelligent than others. The design of Intelligent Quotient (IQ) testing materials meant for the first time there was an attempt to measure students' cognitive abilities and a method to identify a student's potential, rather than merely by summative testing. This, combined with the USA government's desire to keep up with Russian intelligence in the space wars, prompted a higher focus on gifted and talented students. The USA government was beginning to recognise the importance of identifying early students with the potential to excel and creating the right factors for them to do this.

In the 1980s, in response to the raised profile of higher performing students and increased investment from the US government into research, Gagne an American psychologist, designed a model of giftedness and talent (Gagné, 1985). He described a *gift* as a naturally occurring measure of potential which can only be realised through learning, environmental and intrapersonal factors. Once this is realised, then a person with a gift can develop a *talent*.

This was developed further by Harrison (1995) who defined gifted students as '*requiring special provision to meet the needs of their unique abilities and characteristics through social and emotional support from the family, community and educational context*'.

As a result of this clearer definition of gifted and talented students there followed an expectation that schools should be meeting their specific needs. Western governments encouraged schools to maintain gifted and talented registers of their most able students and to improve provision in class for those identified.

Despite these efforts, internationally the provision for gifted and talented students in mainstream education is still developing. Accelerated programmes, enrichment and extracurricular activities have been offered at a wide range of levels, with varying degrees of success. Schools and teachers are still reluctant to triumph the most able students at risk of demotivating others. Teachers are also focusing rightly on the few students at the opposite end of the spectrum – those whose performance is well below that of their peers or of their chronological age. Schools and teachers silently aspire to a community where all students are performing academically at an age-appropriate level and no child is left behind. They choose to focus on the needs of those who are making less progress and not always those who are ahead. This is despite the efforts of governments to raise the profiles of gifted and talented students to improve provision and lift the level of human resources.

Recent research by Geake, J.G. and Gross (2008) found that this discomfort with intellectual advantage is shared across different cultures and nations. Most teachers are reluctant to recognise and improve provision for the intellectually advantaged in the classroom because they view the ability to relate well to others as more important. Further, superior intellectual ability is perceived as a passport to higher education, better employment and a desirable lifestyle by parents and teachers. Policies that single out these students are seen as divisive and promote inequalities.

Investing in training teachers has gone a small way towards changing these views. Also, organisations such as MENSA (www.mensa.org.uk) bring together people whose IQ scores are in the top 2%. This has helped to promote high intellectual ability as an attribute to be respected. Its aim to create a society that is non-political and free from all racial and religious distinctions.

In schools, there is still some way to go. It takes a determined, committed and curious teacher to reveal the gift in a student and nurture it into a talent. Some students have the invaluable support of parents who recognise a natural aptitude and provide the support that is separate from a student's schooling. Most schools and teachers continue to believe that all students irrespective of intellectual ability should be entitled to an education that enriches and empowers. If the provision has to be different to meet their specific need, then let it happen. Opportunities may be missed if we fail to provide appropriately a level of challenge for all our students, no matter their IQ.

Questions for CPD sessions on chapter 10 Gifted and Talented.

1. Does identifying pupils in this way increase inequality in the classroom?
2. If you offer each student, the appropriate level of challenge is this seen as inequality?
3. What are your views on 'this discomfort with intellectual advantage?'
4. How do some schools promote inequality?

11. Learning to Learn

How do we learn? There have been many theories of learning from the early behaviourist theories of Watson, Skinner, Bruner to the cognitive, constructivist theories of Vygotsky and Piaget. All trying to make sense of how humans learn. Critics argue that knowing the many theories does not make an effective teacher or a learner more successful.

Recent research in the International Guide to Student Achievement (Anderman, 2013) supports this view. They argue that understanding our learning behaviours, not theories, improves a person's ability to learn. Our overall ability to 'know what to do when we don't know what to do' is much improved by the use of thinking about learning, often termed 'meta-cognition'.

So, what does this all mean for the teacher and learner? It means that the individual behaviours employed by good learners need to be taught in our schools. Students need to know what they need to do to be a good learner. Guy Claxton in his book *Building Learning Power* (Claxton, 2002), details these very effectively.

Resilience is the first behaviour that is observed in students who can learn well. They are the typical students who can easily become absorbed in a task, and become unaware of the passing of time such is their depth of concentration. They are totally absorbed in the activity. Some students are resilient to distractions because they have learned to manage these. To ignore the chatter of students, close by and know to move to a quieter area when they need to focus. Other students notice changes around them and are encouraged to be observant from an early age. Students who notice what's going on are learning. Finally, a student who is a resilient learner perseveres and keeps going when the learning gets tough. They never give up on a task no matter how difficult. Persevering with difficult maths problems ensures you find the solution by trial and error.

Resourcefulness is the second behaviour exhibited in students who make great progress. They are naturally curious and ask questions. They make connections themselves between areas of learning and can imagine or capitalise concepts and ideas. Resourceful students use logic, they infer and deduce from the information given. Finally, they capitalise on what's available and make great use of resources to further their learning.

Students who learn well are **reflective**. They use their reflections to plan ahead, be prepared and typically write lists. They are flexible and can adapt to changes in routines quickly. They reflect on one approach, consider and apply the approach to other contexts. Students who are reflective accept criticism well and use this to learn. They are open to new ideas and willing to change their viewpoint. They know their own strengths, areas to develop and know how they learn.

Finally, students who can work well with others and **reciprocate** are effective and successful. They know when to work alone and when to collaborate. They can listen to and empathise with others. They know when to be self-reliant and when it's important to be sociable. They learn by imitating, copying other's habits and values.

So we have four defined learning behaviours courtesy of the work of Guy Claxton, resilience, reflectiveness, resourcefulness and reciprocity. How can teachers teach this? They need to explicitly explain to students the behaviours, they need to provide environments that develop and foster behaviours, commentate and model.

Great teachers are doing this already, they are commenting on the student who works well despite distractions, they are fostering a curious ethos in classrooms and encouraging students to persevere when the going gets tough. They actively promote deep thinking in the classroom and allow thinking time.

Some schools build resourcefulness in their students by ensuring students ask questions of the teacher and are explicit in making cross curricular links. Reasoning is taught through creative maths problems and reading comprehension develops skills in logic, inference and deduction.

Reflection is routine and influences planning at all levels in the best schools and learners. They are not afraid in these schools to acknowledge mistakes and consider different approaches.

Being reciprocal, willing and able to learn with others and alone is a skill shared by many students. Some schools are capitalising on this and are encouraging students to learn through imitation. Dialogue amongst students is commonplace in forward-thinking classrooms. Collaboration is used effectively by students who know how to use other people's strategies to help solve their own.

Encouraging students to think about learning means creating teachers that know what it takes to be a powerful learner. It may mean a shift away from the traditional theories of learning that have dominated teacher training establishments. Training will have to improve teachers' knowledge of effective learning behaviours, not theories, so that teachers have the practical skills to develop these in all students at all levels.

Questions for CPD sessions on chapter 11 Learning to Learn.

1. Which do you consider most important, resilience or resourcefulness?
2. List practical ways you can embed thinking time, critical thinking and imagination into your classroom?
3. Find some images related to building learning power and discuss ways of using these in your school.

12. Reading for Meaning

A blind poet dictating the text of Paradise Lost to his daughters. Munkậcsy Mihaly (1844-1900) Hungarian National Gallery Budapest.

So, you are reading. You are now less of a minority than 20 years ago. Illiteracy rates have declined globally, youth and adult literacy rates are increasing. This is mainly due to large organisations such as UNESCO[8] working with governments to promote the need for people to be able to read and write. *"Literacy... enables individuals to achieve their goals, to develop their knowledge and potential, and to participate fully in their community and wider society"* (UNESCO, 2023).

However, if you are a woman with a low income, living in Sub-Saharan Africa or South Asia, your chances of being illiterate are among the highest globally. As a result, you know less. This impacts health decisions, nutrition

---

[8] United Nations Educational Cultural and Scientific Organisation

and the well-being of those that you care for. A child born to a mother who can read is 50% more likely to survive past the age of five and be literate than a child who is born to an illiterate mother.

Fortunately, the picture is improving for these mothers too. Access to primary education combined with access to mobile technologies – which bring words and pictures to even the remotest parts of the world – have all contributed to the global increase in literacy rates for the world's population.

This raises the question, what are these newly literate people reading and writing? They are communicating through the written word, but not in the format of the printed word. Books and newspapers are struggling to maintain prominence in a digital age. Social media sites are replacing printed texts. In October 2018 Facebook, the most popular social network site reports 2.27 billion monthly active users. 37% of these are in Asia and 19% in South America. The countries with the highest number of users were India, USA, Indonesia, Brazil and Mexico. In these countries the newly literate are not reading books, they are active on social networking sites and online using easily available hand-held technologies.

The material the new literate consume is now created at the click of a button. There is little or no check on accuracy, legality or decency. We are bombarded with material every second of the day. The speed at which it is transmitted into our inboxes and social media sites give little time for consideration. 'Is this TRUE?'

Reading remains a subconscious act. Once we have mastered the basic skills of decoding the letters and matching them to the sounds to make sense, fluency improves with practice. As a result of being literate, it is VERY difficult NOT to read something. Therefore, we are acquiring messages in our brains without even realising we are reading. Advertises thrive on this and we are influenced on what to buy and where to go by our subconscious reading.

The choices about what we read are increasingly made for us. If we read or order books online, data is stored about our interests. Smart technologies track our previous reading history. Material then 'pops up' based on our previous browsing activities.

Reading widely and making sure we select from beyond what is selected for us, is even more important if we need to broaden our knowledge and understanding of the world. As Dr Seuss is often famously quoted; *"The more that you read, the more things you will know. The more you learn, the more places you'll go."*

The internet is continually redefining what we read and where we find it. *"To be literate today often means being able to use some combination of blogs, wikis, texting, search engines, Facebook, foursquare, Google Docs, Skype, Chrome, iMovie, Contribute, Basecamp, or many other relatively new technologies, including thousands of mobile applications."* (Leu, 2011) (The new literate requires skills that have not been needed previously if they are to make sense; how to locate information, how to determine if that information is valid, how to analyse information from several different sources, and how to succinctly communicate that information to others. The new literate must be proficient with the tools of technology and be critical to the source. Using this they will make cross-cultural connections, build relationships and share information with others – often strangers – through what they read.

Literacy, being able to read and write is now a well-established social practice using social media sites and mobile technologies. It is no longer a skill reserved for a minority of academics, educators and those who enjoy broadening their minds.

Thinking critically about what we read, where its sourced and its authenticity will enable individuals to develop their knowledge and understanding of the world and the people that are in it. Managing multiple streams of simultaneous information and being able to critique, evaluate and respond to texts quickly has never been more important than now. Only this will allow the world's growing literate populations to make a positive contribution to our global society and read well.

Questions for CPD sessions on chapter 12 Reading for Meaning.

1. Are there any disadvantages of being literate?
2. After reading this chapter what are your views on reading fluency and reading speed and how can you develop that?
3. In your classrooms what approaches can you employ to encourage students to read widely?
4. How can you encourage a routine of read, understand and check the validity?

13. Sharing Stories

We love stories, they are the currency of life. Telling tales is good for us as it helps us to become better at dealing with life's problems. Recent brain research indicates that more neurons are fired when we imagine than when we recall facts. Fictional stimuli strengthen and refine our neural pathways.

However, to share stories we need to be part of a group. Through storytelling, we exchange understandings, emotions and connect with one another. There is a symbiotic exchange between the teller and the listener, and this is essential to our well-being. Maslow's famous Hierarchy of Needs (1943) indicates belonging as one of our most important social needs. After basic needs of food, water and safety, we need to belong. Being together in a group makes you feel good; chemicals in our brain, Oxytocin drive our need to be together. It is fundamental to survival; without the need to be part of a group our survival would be doomed.

So, being part of a group sharing stories is essential to our wellbeing. We are wired up to create networks and share narratives. Long ago our sharing of stories was enhanced with the invention of the printing press in the fifteenth century. For the first-time, stories remained the same over many years and were shared quickly across wider networks. The printed word connected networks of people at different times but at fixed locations.

This remained largely unchanged with the invention of the radio, film and TV in the twentieth century. They all delivered sequential narratives, in a prescribed and timely fashion; you waited for the six o'clock news or today's newspaper. TV, press, radio and film connected wider networks of people, in sequential, often simultaneous and timely fashion.

Then came the internet, combining all previous forms of media; text, audio and video. This bombarded our senses of sight and sound and fired our neurons, rapidly creating even larger social networks of multimedia storytelling. Now, every man has a chance to share a story. Wildly varied stories engage audiences that participate in them. We don't merely share stories now we create them. We comment and share instantaneously. The stories create social networks that have no boundaries of time or place. *'Its boundless connectivity and its endless cascade of hyperlinks turned entertainment into a spelunking expedition'.* (Rose, 2012)

Deliberately ambiguous narratives are posted on social media sites. Wide networks of people debate open-ended questions that engage them in the topic. The film, Star Wars created a massive social network by providing stories with an infinite depth of detail and crafted a blur between fact/fiction, author/audience, entertainment/education. In the same way, The Bible created communities of people, although it took a few hundred years to create a network and the deaths of millions along the way.

But is this good for us? The benefits of social networks are many; a global reach, and speedy connections that are rarely costly or intrusive. Sharing our stories requires little effort on Facebook, Twitter, Instagram and Snapchat. Our networks are large, entertaining, informative and selected.

Emerging drawbacks of sharing stories in this way are well documented. The stream of narratives on social media is fast-paced and overwhelming. It promotes a sedentary lifestyle and can be a distraction to other life pursuits. It is addictive. The truth and source of information are not always clear, images posted are lasting and can be damaging to reputations long after the time they were uploaded. Being critically aware is essential.

Most social media sites are nurturing communications where text is king. Nowadays young people are more likely to text than talk. Texting gives more control over the direction of the story; you can be deliberately ambiguous and avoid difficult conversations by changing the subject. Emotions of anger, laughter sarcasm are far more difficult to notice in the text, or are shown as a small emoticon You can choose when to respond. Stories are most likely to be texted.

So, what next? Social media sites will increasingly encourage social commerce. Live streaming and influencer programmes will become more prolific, sharing stories on social networks. Such as the Old Spice after shave advert live online, where a famous footballer answered questions in his shower for a day, to promote the brand. Ask any teen today and they will tell you they want to be a YouTube Influencer when they grow up.

Will audio make a comeback and overtake text-based sites? Podcasts exist but are rarely socially interactive. Audio networks have the advantage of overcoming poor literacy skills and can be used in any language. But will users make the shift? Hiding behind the safety of a text will be a hard habit to break.

Verbal communication is the human races' greatest advantage. We are a social species and sharing stories has never been so prolific as it is today. Sticks and stones may hurt your bones but telling tales won't hurt you.

Questions for CPD sessions on chapter 13 Sharing Stories.

1. Why are stories important in schools?
2. Discuss stories that are important to you.
3. List the benefits of using social media as an educational tool and the pitfalls to be avoided.
4. Consider creating a policy to detail how social media can be used safely in your school.

14. Mathematics in Schools

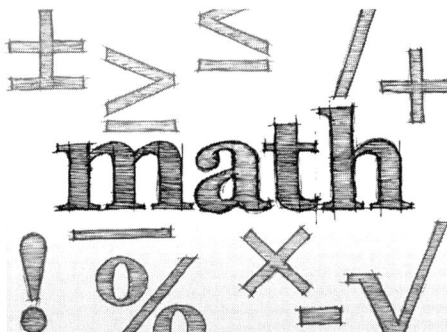

http://creativity103.com/

Do you love it, or do you hate it? Maths is one of those subjects; taught well students perform, taught badly and students fail.

Maths is all around us and in everything we see and do. We cannot avoid mathematical concepts. From the moment we wake up we are calculating; How many more minutes can I have sleeping? How much more money do I need to buy that car? How far is it to the beach? Maths is in the designs and patterns we see, in science, technology and engineering. The architecture of the Lotus Tower in Colombo Sri Lanka is based on mathematical principles concerning loads and structures. Why therefore is maths such a problem for so many people?

The most important factor is that mathematics is hierarchical. If the basic operations of addition, multiplication, subtraction and division are not fully understood in the primary years it is almost impossible to progress to the more complex problems of the secondary curriculum. Understanding the value that a number represents, and its place value is key to all four operations. A gap in any of these areas will impact significantly on the ability to solve other mathematical concepts. The quality of maths teaching in the early years and primary sections is therefore of paramount importance. Receive poor teaching here and it's unlikely that any learner will progress from addition and hate the subject forever.

Mathematical language plays an important part in the learning of mathematical concepts. Yet it is often technical, specific to the subject and not used in everyday life. Further, a teacher cannot teach what a word means. Learners must use and misuse it, try it out, see when it works and how it fits with what they already know. A student teacher commented,

"Some words seem to have different meanings in mathematics, so you get confused."

Mathematics is a sociable subject. If learners are given opportunities to talk and solve problems collaboratively, misconceptions can be eradicated and progress is quicker. An astute teacher realises the benefits of articulation. If a learner can talk about what they are doing, they can complete it independently. Consider then, the benefit of mathematics classes where learners work in silence, individually and talking is seen as a negative.

Further, mathematics requires stamina and perseverance. Finding solutions to problems requires a mixture of logical thinking, detective work and often some inspired trial and error. Eliminating what cannot be true is often a good first step. The fundamental step in the breaking of the Enigma code[9] was the realisation that a letter could not translate into itself, a negative piece of information but of vital importance. Learners need to experience problems that are hard to solve. How will learners ever build up stamina and perseverance if they are only ever given tasks which take

---

[9] The Enigma Code was a way of encrypting messages used by the Germans in world war 2.

seconds, or at best, a few minutes to complete? I once had a student who could work speedily through mathematical problems applying a taught method. This had earned him the reputation of an able mathematician. However, faced with the challenges of Sudoku he failed. He had not learnt the skills to persevere and independently find a solution without being given a method.

Contrary to popular belief, a great mathematician is not always a great teacher. Explaining mathematical concepts requires careful, systematic and appropriate explanations based on the teacher's knowledge of the abilities of each learner. Explaining and considered questioning to check understanding is a skill that not every mathematician may possess.

Frequently mathematical specialist teachers, who lack training in explaining mathematical concepts, may be unwilling to check on the understanding of learners. A student once said of his maths teacher; "I was made to feel like a nuisance for trying to understand. Lots of questions were going around in my head but I was too scared to ask them."

Many good teachers know how to start from building upon prior knowledge, but they are limited in their knowledge of what to do next and frequently a curriculum that is heavily based on content rather than developing thinking. Therefore, learners are given textbooks to work through, individually page-by-page. There is a limited explanation and little check on understanding, other than a summative test at the end of a unit of work.

To produce able mathematicians the quality of teaching is paramount. Brilliant mathematicians throughout history have had mentors. A great mentor or teacher can identify gaps in mathematical understanding and common mathematical misconceptions. They develop skills in abstract thinking, logical reasoning, the application of knowledge to other areas, stamina and perseverance. They engage learners by making connections to the real world and encourage curiosity.

Training teachers to explain mathematical concepts and a curriculum that develops understanding, not rote learning, will give teachers the confidence to be more imaginative in their approaches and engage students. The teaching of mathematics needs to be relevant to the real world, challenging for every student and most of all fun!

Questions for CPD sessions on chapter 14 Mathematics in Schools.

1. How can students be encouraged to work collaboratively in maths?
2. Discuss how self-assessment impacts on progress.
3. Where would you use rote learning in mathematics, is it still important?

15. A Global Education Crisis

https://courses.lumenlearning.com/wm-introductiontosociology/chapter/introduction-to-global-education/

How many children are attending school and yet don't learn? The UN education commission, has turned its attention away from 'schooling' to 'learning'. This is a clear change in focus, from the monitoring of the provision of schools to focusing on the outcomes of learners. Amel Karboul of the United Nations Education Commission described, in a recent TED talk in Milan, an impending Global education crisis: *'330 million children are in school but failing to learn'*. (karboul, October 2017) What does she describe? Karboul describes children who are attending school, but in schools sat a desk receiving teaching but not learning. She adds that combined with this fact there are in addition, 263 million students globally not attending school. If this continues by 2030 half of the world's children and youth will be out of school or not learning.

To begin to get an understanding of the reasons why students in schools are failing to learn, the UN education commission headed by Gordon Brown, the UN special envoy for global education, (Office of the UN Special Envoy for Global Education, 2023) studied the countries where students' achievements exceeded that of others, in standardised assessments. In these countries, students are learning and making progress.

Following a study of the actions of the governments of these countries, the UN commission found a common approach: That where countries track students' progress and make the achievements public, the academic achievement levels for learners improve.

As a result, Karboul argues strongly for all countries to deliver standardised assessments in literacy and numeracy for all students in primary and secondary education. This systematic assessment of learning at the primary and secondary level of all students will give governments the information they need to indicate how many students are learning and the areas of best practice. Kamel believes this close tracking and publication of assessment data is an easy and cost-effective approach to ensure that students are learning. She describes examples of countries such as Vietnam, where rapid progress in learners' achievements has been accomplished through *very close monitoring of students' performances* in standardised assessments and publication of results at school and grade levels. In these countries, she states, governments know that students are learning.

As a result of the close monitoring in these countries, schools have become more accountable for the progress of their students and governments know students are learning. Schools and teachers now realise that the results of their efforts to teach students will be made public.

But what are they learning? What exactly is being tracked? A concern is that this monitoring is focusing only on academic standards. It does not consider other important aspects of learning that take place when students attend school. The indirect and absorbed learning. The personal, social and emotional aspects that are acquired by learners who attend school.

When students attend school, they learn to communicate, to listen as part of a group and ask questions in turn. They learn how to follow instructions. They learn to be independent, to be resilient, know when to ask for help and when it's not appropriate. Students develop self-confidence and self-awareness. They learn to manage their feelings and behaviour in different situations. Where schools facilitate this effectively students follow routines, make relationships and collaborate to solve problems. Most of this may be done in the school playground but students are learning. They are learning increasingly valuable life skills of communication, collaboration and critical thinking through social interaction. There may be many students in schools failing to learn academically but we must not forget the other very important aspects of schooling. Students who have well-developed communication, personal, social and emotional skills, will have greater chances of being successful in life, whether they have the academic qualifications or not.

These skills are not always taught directly by teachers and school leaders, they are facilitated, they are monitored informally by caring committed teachers and guidance is given. Great teachers support students to resolve playground issues and advise students who require more strategies.

Many countries have yet to introduce standardised assessments in literacy and mathematics for all students in every school. Governments do need to ensure students are attending school and that in school they are learning. But they also need to consider what they choose to measure and how. Only when this is implemented will stakeholders know whether attendance in school is making a difference and whether students are learning, or not.

Questions for CPD sessions on chapter 15 A Global Education Crisis.

1. Tracking students' attainment is the only way to success, discuss.
2. Explain the difference between the terms, *attainment, progress* and *achievement.*
3. Students learn just as much in the playground as they do in the classroom, do you agree?
4. Schools should provide for everyone, not just the academically able. Discuss.

16. Communicative Competence or Monolingual Mastery?

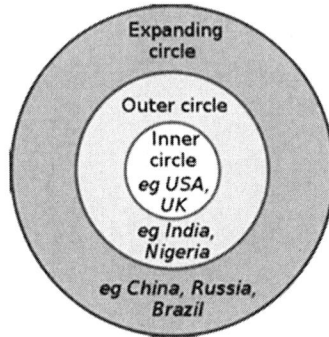

https://commons.wikimedia.org/wiki/File:Kachru%27s_three_
circles_of_English.svg

I am sitting in Dubai. The people around me are all speaking English. Almost all of them are speaking English as a second language from a wide variety of backgrounds, Filipinos, Pakistanis, Indians, and a few Sri Lankans. All communicating effectively in a local variety of English as a common language. Second language speakers of English now referred to as L2, now outnumber first Language speakers of English, L1 by 3:1. Approximately 25% of the world's population speak English, the majority of these using English as a second language, L2.

It is undisputed that English is now an international language. Those that speak it as a second language have been motivated to do so by social and economic factors. We see this on the beaches of Sri Lanka where local traders, often with little formal education, negotiate deals in English and often many other languages. They have been motivated by the need to secure an income from the sale of their goods to tourists. Due to economies of need, they have enhanced skills in communicating.

They communicate by negotiation, by considering the vocabulary needed to ensure the meaning is communicated. They ignore errors and keep lines of communication open, using body language, repetition and careful use of time to engage the customer. They know how to manipulate a dialogue and rely upon key phrases and context. These people have successfully developed a repertoire of communicative competencies that reap financial rewards. Communicative competence does not aim for monolingual perfection. It aims for communication of meaning and understanding.

What does all this mean for education? The belief that the use of standard English as the only possible medium of international and intercultural communication is outdated. Where English is used as a common language, it has developed its own variety relevant to the local culture and context. For example, on the streets of Colombo we regularly hear the use of 'no' to mean 'yes' and directions, 'right side' and 'left side' in three-wheelers. Even though standard English has its own peculiarities, World Englishes[10] vary, even amongst Kachru's inner circle (Kachru, 1986), 'norm providing' communities of first language English speakers, such as America and England.

Despite this, educational institutions continue to promote pedagogic principles that favour standardised English. First language English teachers are employed in preference to teachers who speak English as a second language, irrespective of ability. Multiculturalism is largely ignored in English language teaching curriculums. Most teachers, both L1 and L2, show a preference for standardised English, possibly based on the

---

[10] World Englishes refers to the many different forms and varieties of English spoken throughout the world.

educational experiences they received and the need to pass exams. Monolingual, mastery of standardised English dominates and in many countries the grammar-translation method of teaching is still favoured.

Government policymakers, educational institutions and teachers now need to reconsider the purpose of their English curriculums. If the aim is to ensure students are equipped with the skills to be economically and socially successful, then teachers need to be trained to move away from the standard English L1 model and teach students to have communicative competencies. As Kachru stated in 1992, educational practitioners must now focus on *'facilitating intercultural communicative competence in multilingual and multicultural contexts, rather than idealised mastery of standard English'*. Only then we will be equipping the workforce of the future with the skills they need to be successful.

Suresh Canagarajah (2013), a leading applied linguistics professor, argues that even in academic spheres students should be allowed to write in a style that reflects their cultural identity and use of English. He calls this Translingual Practice. This challenges traditional approaches and promotes serious reconsideration of the use of English in a globalised world. As Canagarajah explains translingualism is not new. People have always had the ability to shuttle between languages. It was the arrival of the colonial powers in South Asia who were keen to create a monolingual standard that brought in the dominance and mastery of one language.

English remains the international language but as varieties evolve relevant to cultures and context, students need to learn to become competent in communicative practices. Nowhere is it more significant than in emerging economies. A shared understanding is a key to a harmonious society where everyone feels they can contribute and be understood. Everyone needs to feel they have a voice. In Dubai, I see communicative competencies at work every day. People shuttling between their own language and a local English variety.

As yet educational establishments at all levels are still bound by the confines of outdated curriculums. They must reconsider their purpose and the needs of the learners. Are teachers aiming for their students to acquire a monolingual mastery of English or a communicative competency?

Questions for CPD sessions on chapter 16 Communicative Competence or Monolingual Mastery?

1. English is used as a method of communication for most of the world's population. Discuss the implications of this.
2. One way to equip students to be economically and socially successful is to be competent in a language. What are other ways?
3. What is the future of language teaching? If the translingual approach is the way forward, how would you support that in your lessons?

17. Online Learning

Open Educational Resources

UNESCO OER Logos

Online learning, e-Learning, networked learning, virtual learning and web-based learning are terms in use that describe how learners use some form of electronic technology to access learning materials and resources. Typically learning is flexible, not fixed to a time or place and the tutor is remote.

This is an extension of the traditional form of distance education that began in the 1900s. Initially, postal courses offered opportunities for study over long distances, followed by advances in broadcasting so that educational materials could be communicated via radio, television, video and teleconferencing. Now we have intelligent databased-assisted learning technologies, webinars, and email, Moodle's, social media platforms, mobile apps and many more. These distance learning tools continue to increase and create a wide breadth of choice for students, teachers, and governments.

This approach to learning is rapidly replacing traditional forms of classroom-based education. It is due largely to the fact that learning online removes constraints of time and distance and offers a great deal of flexibility for students. The most up-to-date materials and experts in the field can be accessed through online learning communities and research (Anderson, 2008) shows that there is no significant difference in the outcomes for learners who learn online in comparison with those who follow traditional lecture-style, classroom-based methods.

Surprisingly, despite all these advantages, the global eLearning market was in steep decline before the global pandemic (Chang, 2016). Free or relatively inexpensive sharing of information and resources was available and there has since been a significant uptake of these. Non-profit organisations such as the Gates Foundation and Hewlitt Foundation are developing educational content that can be open sourced and made available to educational institutions for a free or nominal cost. The American Federation of Teachers (AFT) 2012 created 'share my lesson' a free learning platform and has over 900,000 members. The UK's Times Educational Supplement (TES) hosts a dynamic marketplace in which educators can discover, share and sell original teaching materials. Blendspace is a lesson-building product and wikispaces and social media platforms facilitate teachers' interaction. All offering information transfer in educational communities that is free or affordable. Also, due in part to pressure from consumers who are becoming increasingly aware of lower production costs, digital versions of products are now at prices below their print versions. This further facilitates the ease of transfer of knowledge. Even this publication will be made available as a podcast.

Combined with the availability of free material online highly effective products that promote the transfer of knowledge have also appeared in the marketplace. Mobile learning products, such as game and simulation-based learning applications and cognitive learning products are being rapidly adopted due to lower costs and ease of use by consumers. These mobile learning products are far more effective in the transfer of knowledge and teaching of skills. Further in more advanced applications, psychometric measurement tools quantify their impact. These are replacing online learning courseware, (where the learning is self-paced and in isolation with little or no measure of impact,) at much less cost.

Game-based learning apps have seen the biggest increase, these effectively engage the users' affective and cognitive processes. One successful use is by corporate institutions as part of recruitment processes where game-based scenarios assess cognitive and personality traits using a series of fun and quick neuroscience games. These are cheap, quick, and easy to access.

However, it is the market for students aged 5-12 years that is showing the biggest take up of mobile applications. The Age of learning, ABC Mouse App consistently ranks among the top best-selling education apps. In 2015, 500 children gave their views on virtual reality and e-learning (Insight, n.d.). 79% were aware of virtual reality, 64% wanted virtual reality apps to allow them to visit another country, 64% wanted to visit a place that was not real, 62% wanted to travel on an adventure and 58% asked to travel back in time. This valuable market research will help to provide material that is engaging and attractive to young learners.

Google expeditions is an app that allows students to visit areas without leaving their classrooms. A variety of field trips can be downloaded, and students experience the trip simultaneously, which fosters discussion and analysis. This was used by over 100,000 school age students in 2015.

We are facing a new revolution, characterised by innovation, highly effective transfer of knowledge and learning. As consumers move rapidly towards mobile applications which are easy to use and affordable, we are seeing a 'leapfrog effect', particularly in the developing world where communities can bypass the PC based online learning systems in favour of the new mobile technologies, as is the case in Sri Lanka. The rapidly advancing market is driven by consumer demand for low costs, ease of access and attractive content. However, there is a danger that we are narrowing choices rather than broadening them and there is a fear that careful consideration of what the learner needs, has been forgotten.

Questions for CPD sessions on chapter 17 Online Learning.

1. Is the future of schools online? Discuss the implications of this for students.
2. How is online learning narrowing curriculum choices?
3. Can we trust free online lessons and schemes of work? Who is regulating the online resources?
4. Technology will allow more people to access education. Discuss the impact and disadvantages of this.

18. Risk-Taking and Creativity

You cannot be creative without taking a risk. When producing something new, unusual and innovative there is always the chance of failure, that the creation may not produce the intended results. Risk-taking and creativity are interdependent, they cannot exist without each other.

As children, we take risks, we learn through making mistakes in climbing trees, solving problems and making new friendships. Children explore unknown worlds, interacting freely with one another through stories and role play, building imaginary towers and reconstructing them. Children brought up in trusted environments knowing they can make mistakes without fear of failure, will feel free to explore and be creative.

As a young mother, I took my children to an art exhibition. Whilst walking around and looking at the artworks by an established artist, my son, then aged three commented loudly and in earshot of the artist, "They're not as good as mine, are they, Mummy?" My son was not unusual. Children are wonderfully egocentric and believe fully in the validity and usefulness of their own creations.

Unfortunately, as adults, most of us become more self-aware and conscious of the mistakes that we make and how they may be perceived by others. We lose the ability to take risks for fear of failure, we abide by the rules and compare our creative efforts against the work of others. It is rare for an adult to believe fully in the validity and usefulness of their own creations, in fact, other adults would term this arrogance. And as a result, our creativity declines. Through fear of failure and the need to conform we embed these unspoken rules into our children. Here is an example of how parents indirectly instil these rules into their children at a very early age.

Whilst working to develop nursery students' language skills in an English medium preschool, I strongly advocated the use of role play. The teachers were easily convinced and worked hard to establish an outdoor petrol shed made from cardboard boxes and used old car tyres. However, the students – when presented with the petrol shed play area – did not play. They observed; politely. The unspoken rule that school was a place to learn and not play had been instilled into them from an early age. Here we had a situation where the teachers were breaking the rules, taking the risks and the students did not know what to do. School was a place to work, abide by the rules and not play. So, teachers taking the initiative became role models and played; this encouraged a few girls who started to play at the desk, serve imaginary petrol and write out bills. Gradually the boys joined in, taking the cardboard cars to the pumps, speaking in their mother tongue and English. Initially, the play was reserved and stilted, but these young students soon overcame their fears to play in school, and the languages of both English and mother tongue flourished.

Having the confidence to act independently, try out new ideas and not be frightened of failure is an important skill that we lose with age. Placing adults into imaginary worlds enables them to empathise. Like children, adults dressing up as firefighters in training sessions, helps them to imagine what it feels like to speak and act as a firefighter.

To be creative, you need to be able to explore the possibilities, look beyond what everybody else is doing, be imaginative. Not only acting but also constructing, thinking with your hands, making and remaking. Many new designs have been created using paper clips, sticky tape and film canisters and failed at first. Eames (Renauld, 2020), a furniture designer discovered the endless opportunities that plywood could be put to, through exploring designs that went beyond the norm. The roll-on deodorant eventually became the computer mouse. A teacher, whilst working with a team of NGOs, made playdough from rice flour for use in schools, which was later attached to detonators to aid the demining of Cambodia.

"The biggest risk is not taking any," said Mark Zuckerberg in an interview in 2016 (Zuckerman, 2016). If we don't take risks because we are afraid to make a mistake we will never learn. We need to shock people out of normal thinking. Poverty, lack of resources and desperation do this, they force people to become divergent thinkers and often the people with the most creative ideas are the most desperate.

If we can retain some of the free-thinking, risk-taking, ego-centric characteristics we possess as children and begin to explore questions such as… what if? Then there is a chance that creativity will remain with us and enable our survival for years to come. Our survival depends upon us being imaginative, asking questions and never being afraid to fail.

Keep thinking outside the box.

Questions for CPD sessions on chapter 18 Risk Taking and Creativity.

1. There is no creativity without risk. Discuss.
2. How can you encourage more risk taking within your subject area?
3. At what age do you stop being imaginative? If we as adults are creative and imaginative how will this impact on our students?
4. The poorest people are often the most creative. Do you agree?

Bibliography

Ambientinsight.com, n.d. Ambient Insight. [Online] Available at: https://sur.ly/i/ambientinsight.com/.

Anderman, E. M. H. J., 2013. International Guide to Student Achievement. 1st ed. New York: Routledge.

Anderson, T., 2008. The Theory and Practice of Online Learning. Second Edition Canada: Athabasca University Press.

Anon., n.d. American Federation of Teachers. [Online] Available at: https://www.aft.org/ [Accessed 2023].

Argaez, E. d., 2022. https://internetworldstats.com/facebook.htm. [Accessed January 2023].

Benjamin, L., 1988. A history of teaching machines. American Psychologist, pp. Vol 43 703-712.

Britannica, E., n.d. https://www.britannica.com. [Online] Available at: https://www.britannica.com/biography/Mark-Zuckerberg

Canagarajah, S. (2012). Translingual Practice: Global Englishes and Cosmopolitan Relations (1st ed.). Routledge.

Chandler, J. G., 1840. The Remarkable Story of Chicken Little

Chang, R., 2016. The Journal. [Online] Available at:
https://thejournal.com/articles/2016/09/01/global-
elearning[1]market[1]insteep-decline.aspx [Accessed January 2023]

Claxton, G., 2002. Building Learning Power. 1st ed. Bristol: TLO Ltd.
Commission, E., 2016.

Commission, E., 2016.The Learning Generation, an executive summary.
[Online] Available at: https://report.educationcommission.org/report/
[Accessed January 2023].

DfE UK, 2011. Teachers Standards Available at:
https://www.gov.uk/government/publications/teachersstandards [Accessed
25 December 2022].

DfE, 2015. Short-breaks-damage-young-peoples-futures Press release.
[Online] Available at: https://www.gov.uk/government/news/short-breaks-
damage-youngpeoples-futures [Accessed 10 January 2023]

Ferguson, N.M., Earley, P., Fidler, B., & Ouston, J. (2000). Improving
Schools and Inspection: The Self-Inspecting School.

Fisher, R., 2013. Teaching Thinking. Philosophical Enquiry in the
Classroom. 4th ed. London: Bloomsbury.

Foundation, E. E., 2022. Teaching-Learning-Toolkit. [Online] Available at:
https://educationendowmentfoundation.org.uk/education[1]evidence/using
the-toolkits [Accessed January 2023].

Foundation, H., n.d. Hewlett.org. [Online] Available at: https://hewlett.org/ [Accessed 2023].

Frank Rose, 2011. Wired. [Online] Available at: https://www.wired.com/2011/03/star-wars-generation/[Accessed 30 December 2022]

Gagné, F., 1985. Giftedness and talent: Re-examining; a re-examination of the definitions. Gifted Child Quarterly, 29 (3), 103–112., 29(3), pp. 103-112.

Gagné, F., 1999. My Convictions About the Nature of Abilities, Gifts, and Talents. Journal for the Education of the Gifted, 22(2), 109–136., 22(2), p. 109–136.

Gates, B. &.M., n.d. Gatesfoundation.org/. [Online] Available at: https://www.gatesfoundation.org/ [Accessed 2023].

Geake, J.G. and Gross., 2008. Teachers' Negative Affect Toward Academically Gifted Students. Gifted Child Quarterly 52, (3), p. pp. 217–231. 89

Harrison, C. (1995). Giftedness in Early Childhood. KU Children's Services.

Hart Research Associates, 2013. It takes more than a major:
[Online] Available at:
https://dgmg81phhvh63.cloudfront.net/content/userphotos/Research/PDFs /2013_EmployerSurvey.pdf [Accessed 11 January 2023

Hattie, J., 2008. Visible Learning. 1st ed. Melbourne: Routledge.

HMSO, 1992. Education (Schools) Act, London: Her Majesty's Stationery Office.

Insight, A., n.d. Ambient Insight.com. [Online] Available at: https://sur.ly/i/ambientinsight.com/.

Kachru, B. B., 1986. The Alchemy of English. Oxford: Pergamon Press Oxford.

Karboul, A., October 2017. The Global Learning Crisis and What to do about it. Milan: TED Talks.

Learning_Generation_Full_Report.pdf (2015)
https://report.educationcommission.org. Available at:
https://report.educationcommission.org/wpcontent/uploads/2016/09/Learning_Generation_Full_Report.pdf (Accessed: January 10, 2., n.d. [Online].

Lemov, D., 2010. 49 Techniques that Put Students on the Path to College. 1st ed. ed. s.l.: Jossey-Bass.

Leu, D.J., Gregory McVerry, J., Ian O'Byrne, W., Kiili, C., Zawilinski, L., Everett-Cacopardo, H., Kennedy, C. and Forzani, E. (2011), The New Literacies of Online Reading Comprehension: Expanding the Literacy and Learning Curriculum. Journal of Adolescent & Adult, 55(1), pp. 5-14.

Macbeath, J., 2006. School Inspection & Self-Evaluation: Working with the New Relationship. 1st edition. Routledge

Maslow, 1943. A Theory of Human Motivation. Psychological Review, 50(4), pp. 370-396.

MENSA.org, n.d. MENSA. [Online] Available at: https://mensa.org.uk/

Montague, A., 1966. On Being Human. New and revised edition ed. New York: Hawthorn Books.

New York Times, 2009. President Obama's Remarks to the Hispanic Chamber of Commerce.

[Online] Available at:
https://www.nytimes.com/2009/03/10/us/politics/10textobama.html
[Accessed January 2023].

OECD, n.d. Programme for International Student Assessment. [Online] Available at: https://www.oecd.org/pisa/

Office of the UN Special Envoy for Global Education, 2023. Who we are and what we do: Gordon Brown. [Online] Available at:
https://educationenvoy.org/what-we-do/ [Accessed January 2023].

Ofsted, 2019. Ofsted Education inspection framework. [Online] Available at:
https://www.gov.uk/government/collections/education-inspection/framework [Accessed January 2023].

Ogilvy, D., 1985. Ogilvy on advertising. 1st edition New York: Vintage Books.

Renauld, M., 2020. The Collector. [Online] Available at:
https://www.thecollector.com/charles-and-ray-eames-furniturearchitecture-contributions/ [Accessed 27 Dec 2022].

Robinson, A., 2013. A Century of Contributions to Gifted Education: Illuminating Lives. 1st ed. Routledge.

Rose, F., 2012. The Art of Immersion: How the Digital Generation Is Remaking Hollywood, Madison Avenue, and the Way We Tell Stories. 1st ed. New York: W.W. Norton & co.

Schultz, H. &.D. Y., 1997. Pour Your Heart into It: How Starbucks Built a Company One Cup at a Time. 1st paperback ed. New York: Hyperion.

Shimazoe, J. a. H. A., 2010. Group Work Can Be Gratifying: Understanding & Overcoming Resistance to Cooperative Learning. College Teaching, vol. 58, no. 2, (http://www.jstor.org/stable/25763419), p. 52–57.

College Teaching, vol. 58, no. 2, (http://www.jstor.org/stable/25763419), p. 52–57.

Taylor, C., 2012. Improving attendance at School, London: Crown Copyright.

Toffler, A., 1971. Future Shock. Paperback ed. Bantam.

UNESCO, 2017. Global Education Monitoring Report Accountability in Education, Paris France: United Nations.

UNESCO, 2023. UNESCO Institute for statistics Definition. [Online] Available at: http://uis.unesco.org/en/glossary-term/literacy [Accessed January 2023].

UNICEF, 1989. United Nations Convention on the Rights of the Child. [Online] Available at: https://www.unicef.org.uk/wpcontent/uploads/2019/10/UNCRC_summary -1_1.pdf [Accessed January 2023]

Unknown, n.d. National Archives UK. [Online] Available at: https://www.nationalarchives.gov.uk/ [Accessed 2023].

Ventura, M., Lai, E., & DiCerbo, K. (2017) 2017. Skills for Today: What We Know about Teaching and Assessment, London: Pearson.

Zuckerman, M., 2016. How to build the future [Interview] (September 2016).